HERMANN'

C000000361

Everything You Need To Know
About Hermann's Tortoise. How
To Care, Feed, House, Growth,
Life Span, Health Care And How
They Make Amazing Pet

MARK ANDERSON

Table of Contents

CHAPTER ONE

INTRODUCTION

Hermann's tortoise—alongside the spur-thighed tortoise and the marginated tortoise—is a part of a set of tortoises called "Mediterranean tortoises." This attractive tortoise, with a yellow and brown carapace, thick scales, and robust legs, is quite coveted for its slight temperament and its sheer splendor. Inside the wild, Hermann's tortoises live in rocky hillsides and all right and beech forests of the Mediterranean place of Europe. However, due to habitat loss, falling victim to road kill, and over-collection for the pet enterprise, each the Western Hermann's tortoises and Jap Hermann's tortoises are nearing endangerment. That said, captive breeding and conservation efforts have had a superb impact on repopulating the species.

The passive and gentle Hermann's tortoise makes a terrific puppy for the right person who lives in an appropriate climate with plenty of outside area. This active creature loves to run (surprisingly), dig, forage, climb, and sunbathe. Male tortoises frequently have interaction and might interact in combat, particularly for the duration of the mating seasons of spring and fall. All through courtship, male tortoises excessively chase and ram the females, every now and then inflicting damage. For this reason, it's miles excellent to residence men and women one at a time to avoid damage, bringing them collectively handiest to mate.

CHAPTER TWO

HOUSING THE HERMANN'S TORTOISE

Hermann's tortoises do now fare nicely in house (interior). So preserve this in mind earlier than buying one. And because outside housing is strongly endorsed, make certain you stay in a climate that carefully mimics that of the Mediterranean (Italy, Greece, Bulgaria, and Romania). daylight temperatures must average around 80 to 86 degrees Fahrenheit (27 to 30 stages Celsius) and should not fall under

65 to 70 tiers Fahrenheit (18 to 21 ranges Celsius) at night. Tortoise habitats need to include a shallow pan of water (preferably sunk into the ground), rocks, small trees and timber, and a refuge to shield it from severe weather and predators. The pen must additionally be get away-evidence on account that these lively tortoises tend to climb and burrow.

Warmth

If you decide to residence your tortoise indoors, a reasonably big enclosure is vital (a 2- through 4-

foot minimal). offer a basking mild or heat lamp that mimics the solar, complete with a basking spot (flat rocks work properly) that has an ambient temperature of about 95 tiers Fahrenheit (35 tiers Celsius). It's also important to have a groovy, shaded area to your tortoise to break out the warmth.

Substrate

A mix of soil, sand, and composted cypress bark should make up the substrate in your pet's enclosure. The compost aggregate have to be about inches deep so that your tortoise can dig and frolic inside the dust. Burrowing lets in your tortoise to chill itself off, while also supplying a way to thwart boredom. A shallow pan of water should also be supplied for each drinking and cooling off. Make certain to offer one deep sufficient in your puppy to immerse its complete frame.

If the enclosure or outdoor temperature drops fewer than 50 ranges Fahrenheit, your pet tortoise can also determine to hibernate. Some species hibernate inside the wild for as much as 5 months, generally among October and April. For indoor tortoises, however, it's miles tough to maintain the environmental situations conducive to a secure hibernation. Therefore, it is pleasant now not to permit your enclosure temperatures drop to hold your tortoise energetic all yr long.

CHAPTER THREE

WHAT TO FEED HERMANN'S TORTOISE

A tortoise's weight-reduction plan ought to reflect wild foraging. Pick out a variety of leafy greens and grasses to feed your puppy. Then, complement with smaller portions of veggies (broccoli, cabbage, cauliflower, cucumber, and carrots) and fruit (apples, apricots, grapes, melons, peaches, and strawberries). For an indoor tortoise, it's especially vital to ramp up its vitamins since it is not directly exposed to daylight. A tortoise meals, whole with calcium and diet D3, works well. Wild tortoises also devour bugs, slugs, and carrion; however in case you complement with those critters, keep in mind that feeding your pet an excessive amount of animal protein can damage it. And since tortoises are especially vegetarian, never feed your reptile dog or cat food.

CHAPTER FOUR

COMMON HEALTH OF HERMANN'S TORTOISE

All through mating season, turtles get aggressive, so, tortoises must be monitored and inspected day by day for wounds at some point of this crucial time. Take care of all injuries well via first setting apart the injured reptile. Next, smooth the wound and get rid of debris. Then, observe an antibacterial solution like honey and get dressed the wound. Take care in doing so, however, due to the fact tortoises do not like pointless dealing with and the stress should prolong recuperation. Unattended open wounds are liable to contamination and provide a breeding floor for flies and maggots.

Tortoises in captivity also are susceptible to a slew of different illnesses. A breathing contamination can arise in tortoises who've not been nicely cared for. And environmental stresses or lack of fresh meals and easy water can cause a contamination. If you suspect your turtle has a respiratory contamination, take it to your exotics vet. He'll most probable prescribe a round of antibiotics. With right care and desirable living conditions, your tortoise need to enhance, despite the fact that it can take several weeks to 1 month for a full recovery.

Metabolic bone disease can occur in puppy tortoises due to a lack of calcium or trouble absorbing calcium. When you consider that wild turtles bask inside the solar for maximum of the day, a full-spectrum light is wanted in an effort to naturally take in nutrition D (a nutrient required for calcium absorption). Prevention is easy via providing the right conditions and proper vitamins. Nonetheless, if your tortoise indicates signs of this disease—like a tender or misshapen shell—take it to the vet. Situations want to be corrected and liquid calcium might also need to be supplemented.

If dehydration happens, prolapsed of the cloacae can take place when the bladder of the tortoise paperwork a "stone" which the reptile then tries to bypass. If this happens, your vet will assist your pet get rid of the stone and manipulate the organ again interior, sometimes ensuing in a suture to completely heal.

CHAPTER FIVE

THINGS TO CONSIDER WHILE PICKING HERMANN'S TORTOISE AS PET

It's miles satisfactory to shop for your tortoise directly from a breeder, each for the health of the puppy in addition to the survival of the species. Shopping for from a good breeder assures your pet has not been obtained from a supply this is depleting wild populations. Breeders additionally provide super care. Shopping for a Hermann's tortoise from a puppy shop or provider, but, is not endorsed. Sellers might also have received their tortoises from a non-reputable supply and, regularly, the living environment they offer is sub-par, main to a diseased puppy.

A species wherein that is some distance less of a trouble is the Hermann's tortoise. Native to the Mediterranean coasts of southern Europe, this species is noticeably hardy and does now not reach a size greater than about 10 to twelve inches (25-30cm) in length.

In case you are serious about maintaining a tortoise as a pet and you're already familiar with the idiosyncrasies associated with tortoises in fashionable; which includes sturdiness and, regularly at the least, the need to hibernate, then choosing a Hermann's tortoise might be a sensible desire.

That's no longer to say a Hermann's tortoise is a lazy character's puppy but, there's an awful lot to study keeping one, and they nevertheless require a superb deal of care. So please study on before making a decision to buy.

Furthermore, why choosing a Herman tortoise you still have to consider the following:

Length and Weight

Hermann's tortoises are physically much like many different tortoises species, however greater so specially (and unsurprisingly) to other mediterranean species.

Hermann's tortoises are a medium sized breed, with hatchlings being up 1.5 (3.5cm) long, which within reason normal amongst most breeds.

Fully grown girls may reach 10 to twelve inches (25-30cm) in length, even as males have a tendency to be smaller. Likewise a completely grown girl can attain a weight of round eight pounds (3.5kg). Normally but, maximum specimens will no longer reach a size or weight as advanced as this.

Shade and Shell pattern

The top a part of a tortoise's shell is referred to as the carapace, which within the case of a Hermann's tortoise, can vary between sunglasses of organic yellows, greens and browns, whilst the underbelly (plastron) has a tendency to be a faint yellow or bone color with outstanding dark brown or black markings.

The uncovered areas of pores and skin on the head and legs are once more an earthy inexperienced or yellow color. There are normally scaly areas on the legs, probable to guard the limbs when burrowing.

A wholesome Hermann's tortoise may have a surprisingly smooth shell, which appears domed whilst considered from the side. Like all tortoises the shell is a quintessential a part of the tortoise's skeleton, with the outer plates of the shell (referred to as scutes) being an extension of the ribs and spine.

Senses

There may be a few debates approximately how well tortoises are capable of pay attention, but they truly own good eyesight which permits them to track down food that is secure to eat. Hermann's tortoises are no exception, and prefer all other species they have a pointy beak instead of enamel to slice via their food.

You'll seldom hear a tortoise making any kind of sound vocally, however males may additionally grunt and squeak at some stage in dating and mating with a female.

In conjunction with their robust eyesight, tortoises also have an amazing sense of smell. Used in aggregate those two senses again allow a tortoise to tune down meals this is secure to consume.

Limbs

I every now and then assume it seems like difficult work when I see my tortoise hauling himself about the vicinity, almost as though the shell is weighing him down. Possibly for that reason tortoise legs have developed to be a strong as possible for you to shift round the sort of heavy payload.

The rear legs specially resemble those of an elephant, so surely there are a few anatomical similarities amongst tortoises and other heavy animals.

CHAPTER SIX

HOW TO DISTINGUISH BETWEEN MALE AND FEMALE HERMANN'S TORTOISE

One of the trickiest matters for the untrained eye to do is determine the sex of a tortoise. We understand that females are normally larger than adult males; however this isn't especially beneficial for the reason that there are always exceptions, and besides, except you have got more than one tortoise, you received have a point of reference.

The handiest way to get a reasonably accurate idea of the intercourse is by way of staring at the duration of the tail; in men it has a tendency to be a ways longer, lengthy enough to wrap around barely, while a female's tail is much more likely to be stubby.

You're simplest probably to want to recognize for certain whether your tortoise is male or girl if you plan to hold tortoises collectively, in any other case it's a fairly inconsequential detail that won't affect your husbandry.

Internal Anatomy

Even though they look unusual on the outside, tortoises characteristic the identical fundamental inner structures as different vertebrates, including humans. This consists of a digestive tract and a respiration system similar to our personal.

There are of direction diffused variations, consisting of a distinct musculature shape to facilitate the inhalation and exhalation of air; due to the fact not like us, tortoises can't flex and expand their rib cages to allow air to make bigger and fill their lungs.

It's additionally exciting to notice that tortoises have heart made from 3 rather than 4 chambers. This, as you may think, isn't always as effective at circulating blood for the duration of the body, which is going a protracted way closer to explaining why tortoises prefer to take existence at a particularly greater leisurely tempo than we do, and why they speedy tire after quick periods of exertion.

Reproductive gadget

It's fair to mention that the reproductive structures of

tortoises are of specific interest to many humans!

Like other reptiles, birds, and some mammals, tortoises possess cloacae; a multi-reason orifice that serves as each the factor of excretion of urine and stable waste fabric, in addition to the reproductive commencing.

Male tortoises do have a phallus, although it is rarely seen as it's miles stored in the body, only emerging on the point of mating while the male will implant sperm within the lady's cloacae.

Women produce eggs in a good deal the same way as birds and

other reptiles, passing them thru their cloacae while they're equipped.

Hermann's Tortoise conduct

Just as birds are adapted for flight, and penguins are tailored to low temperatures, Hermann's tortoises have particular organic and behavioral adaptations that allow them to thrive in their herbal habitat.

It's important to have knowledge of those adoptions so that you can do your satisfactory to simulate

the best surroundings to your pet Hermann's to thrive in.

CHAPTER SEVEN

GROWTH AND LIFESPAN OF A HERMANN'S TORTOISE

Hermann's tortoises are slower developing than some of their larger cousins, usually taking about a decade to attain adulthood and their absolutely grown size. Again, this may be up to 12" (30cm) but around 10" (25cm) is an awful lot extra regular.

It's crucial no longer to strive and expedite the growth of your tortoise in any manner (by using feeding them meat for instance)

because this will result in problems inclusive of the frame developing too quick and outgrowing the shell, main to all varieties of health troubles. Certainly, one of the key motives behind hibernation is to slow down the growth process of the tortoise.

A Hermann's tortoise will stay for something between 50 and 75 years if nicely cared for, although inside the wild many do no longer reach such a sophisticated age due to predation and illness.

Pores and skin and Scute dropping

A lesser known system exhibited by way of tortoises is the persistent dropping of their skin and shell scutes. Not like a reptile such as a snake that sheds all of its pores and skin in one move, tortoises (much like us in lots of ways) usually shed their skin such that it isn't especially substantive.

I haven't individually witnessed the dropping of shell scutes, being a less ordinary exercise than pores and skin losing, however it does none the less manifest.

Metabolism and Digestion

Like different reptiles, tortoises are a cold blooded animal that means their inner temperature is entirely established upon the temperature in their environment; unlike mammals that are capable of self alter their inner temperature until ambient temperatures are dangerously excessive or low.

In any case, this indicates a tortoise's metabolism may be faster while the air is warmer, at the same time as at cold temperatures their physical features gradual proper down.

Each states serve their motive, as an instance at hotter temperatures they're able to digest meals more efficiently, at the same time as a constantly low temperature gives the proper situations for hibernation.

CHAPTER EIGHT

FORAGING AND FEEDING BEHAVIOR OF HERMANN'S TORTOISE

Like maximum tortoises, Hermann's tortoises are herbivorous (although I've witnessed one consume a slug on more than one event). In their herbal habitat Hermann's tortoises will forage for meals in the course of the day, however, they prefer to devour early in the day whilst the air is cooler. Presumably this corresponds with digestion taking vicinity slightly later whilst the air is hotter. It additionally manner they could keep out of the warmth by chickening out to a sheltered region, far away from the noon solar with a belly full of food to maintain them going.

Whilst temperatures drop later in the afternoon, tortoises may fit for a 2d round of foraging, even though they received it in all likelihood eat as an awful lot as food may be digested greater slowly in the decrease middle of the night temperature.

Like other hibernating species of tortoise, Hermann's tortoises will choose to hibernate when temperatures continually drop below a positive degree (generally 2°F-10°C or 35.6°-50°F).

Within the wild they will find a safe burrow or crevice to sleep in during the wintry weather; however they are more than capable of wake briefly for a time if the temperature reaches an uncharacteristically high parent throughout 12 months.

Protecting Behavior

Tortoises aren't evidently aggressive animals, and depend

commonly on being inconspicuous to try to keep away from disagreement with predators. This involves taking advantage of their herbal camouflage and by using burrowing.

Mature specimens have the defense of a hard shell that is difficult to break for most small predatory mammals, and of direction the tortoise will retract its limbs and head into its shell while immediate threat is detected.

More youthful tortoises don't have a completely hardened shell but, so it's even extra important for them to maintain properly out of sight unless foraging.

THE END

Printed in Great Britain
by Amazon

40482395R00030